Exam FA2
Maintaining Financial Records

Pocket Notes

British library cataloguing-in-publication data

A catalogue record for this book is available from the British Library.

Published by:
Kaplan Publishing UK
Unit 2 The Business Centre
Molly Millars Lane
Wokingham
Berkshire
RG41 2QZ

ISBN 978-1-78740-425-0

© Kaplan Financial Limited, 2019

Printed and bound in Great Britain.

The text in this material and any others made available by any Kaplan Group company does not amount to advice on a particular matter and should not be taken as such. No reliance should be placed on the content as the basis for any investment or other decision or in connection with any advice given to third parties. Please consult your appropriate professional adviser as necessary. Kaplan Publishing Limited and all other Kaplan group companies expressly disclaim all liability to any person in respect of any losses or other claims, whether direct, indirect, incidental, consequential or otherwise arising in relation to the use of such materials.

All rights reserved. No part of this publication may be reproduced, stored in a retrieval system, or transmitted, in any form or by any means, electronic, mechanical, photocopying, recording or otherwise, without the prior written permission of Kaplan Publishing.

Contents

Chapter 1	Recording transactions	1
Chapter 2	Trial balance	21
Chapter 3	Final accounts – introduction and accounting policies	31
Chapter 4	Non-current assets	39
Chapter 5	Control account reconciliations	53
Chapter 6	Bank reconciliation	61
Chapter 7	Accruals, prepayments and irrecoverable debts	69
Chapter 8	Closing inventory, liabilities and provisions	79
Chapter 9	Extended trial balance	89
Chapter 10	Sole trader accounts	95
Chapter 11	Partnership accounts	105
Chapter 12	Incomplete records	115
Index		I.1

Preface

These Pocket Notes contain everything you need to know for the exam, presented in a unique visual way that makes revision easy and effective.

Written by experienced lecturers and authors, these Pocket Notes break down content into manageable chunks to maximise your concentration.

Quality and accuracy are of the utmost importance to us so if you spot an error in any of our products, please send an email to mykaplanreporting@kaplan.com with full details, or follow the link to the feedback form in MyKaplan.

Our Quality Co-ordinator will work with our technical team to verify the error and take action to ensure it is corrected in future editions.

Introduction

In this chapter

- Overview of the examination.
- Keys syllabus areas.

Overview of the examination

This examination will consist of:

50 compulsory objective test questions for two marks each	100
Total marks	100

The examination duration is two hours. The pass mark is 50%.

The examination is available as a computer-based examination.

As the examination consists entirely of objective test questions, you do need to consider the following:

- Objective test questions allow the examiner to cover a significant amount of the syllabus within each examination. This means you cannot simply learn only part of the syllabus and hope to achieve a pass standard – you will need to learn the entire syllabus to maximise your chances of success in the examination.

- As part of your revision, work through the questions in the study text and any question banks you may have to ensure you understand the style of question asked.

- You should ensure that you allocate your time correctly so that you can answer all questions.

- Remember in the examination, you can answer questions in any order (as long as you complete the objective test correctly. It is therefore worth completing the easier questions first and then re-visiting the more difficult questions before the end of the examination. This approach will (hopefully) ensure you have obtained the easy marks first and avoid missing them should you run out of time.

Finally, when all else fails, guess – there is no negative marking.

Introduction

Objective test question styles

- Multiple choice – where you are required to choose one answer from a list of options provided by clicking on the appropriate 'radio button'
- Multiple response – where you are required to select more than one response from the options provided by clicking on the appropriate tick boxes(typically choose two options from the available list
- Multiple response matching – where you are required to indicate a response to a number of related statements by clicking on the 'radio button' which corresponds to the appropriate response for each statement
- Number entry – where you are required to key in a response to a question shown on the screen

Key syllabus areas

The aim of FA2 is to develop knowledge and understanding of the underlying principles and concepts relating to Maintaining Financial Records and technical proficiency in the use of double-entry accounting techniques including the preparation of basic financial statements.

On completion of FA2 candidates should be able to:

- Explain generally accepted accounting principles and concepts.
- Outline the principles and process of basic bookkeeping.
- Preparing journals and ledger accounts.
- Record transactions and events.
- Prepare a trial balance (including identifying and correcting errors).
- Reconcile the control accounts and cashbook.
- Extend the trial balance, including year-end adjustments and final accounts.
- Account for partnerships.

chapter

1

Recording transactions

In this chapter

- Basic recording of business transactions.
- Key accounts in financial statements.
- General ledger.
- Credit transactions and sales tax.
- Ledgers – key definitions.
- Discounts.
- Purchases cycle.
- Cash payments cycle.
- Sales cycle.
- Variable consideration.
- Cash receipts cycle.
- Journal.

Basic recording of business transactions

Key Point

Business entity concept = a business is separate from its owners. The owner's private transactions are not entered in the business' books.

An entity may be a sole trader, a partnership, a limited company or a non-profit making organisation.

Exam focus

Only sole traders and partnerships are examinable within FA2.

Accounting

- Records a business' transactions.
- Summarises the transactions.

The accounting equation

Assets
- Land and buildings
- Plant and machinery
- Motor vehicles
- Inventory
- Money in bank
- Receivables

=

Liabilities
- Payables
- Bank loan
- Bank overdraft
- Other payables (e.g. tax due to tax authorities)

+

Capital
- Amounts introduced to business by owner.

- Accounting equation elements change over time (e.g. a cash sale results in a fall in inventory and an increase in cash).
- Despite this, the equation will always balance = basis of double entry bookkeeping.
- All transactions are entered into the accounts twice – a debit and a credit.
- Sum of all debits = sum of all credits.

Example

A new business is involved in the following tranactions:

1. The owner injects $4,000 capital into the business
2. $1,500 is spent purchasing goods for resale
3. $2,000 is spent purchasing land
4. Another $1,500 goods for resale are acquired on credit

After these transactions, the accounting equation is as follows:

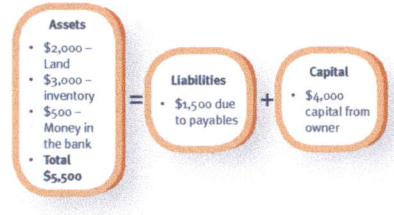

Key accounts in financial statements

Statement of profit or loss:

- Shows financial performance for business for one period of time (normally 12 months)
- Revenue = amounts obtained from selling goods and services
- Expenses = costs incurred in providing goods / services
- Profit = difference between revenue and expenses. It is transferred to the balance sheet.

Key Point

The statement of profit or loss shows performance over a period of time; the statement of financial position shows position at one point in time.

Revenue
- Sales of goods/services less sales returns

−

Expenses
- Cost of goods sold
- Salaries
- Telephone
- Rent
- Light, heat and power
- Interest on bank loan, etc

=

Profit
- Surplus over expenses paid
- Can be negative – indicates 'loss'

Statement of financial position

- Shows overall financial position of business at a particular date in time
- Assets = something owned or controlled by the business
- Liabilities = amounts owed by business to third parties
- Assets and liabilities can be current or non-current (payable in more than one year)
- Capital = owner's investment + (-) all profits (losses) to date – all drawings to date
- Drawings = amounts of cash withdrawn from the business by the owner.

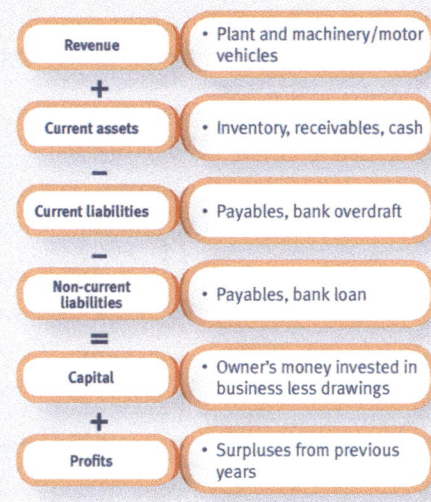

Revenue	Plant and machinery/motor vehicles
+	
Current assets	Inventory, receivables, cash
−	
Current liabilities	Payables, bank overdraft
−	
Non-current liabilities	Payables, bank loan
=	
Capital	Owner's money invested in business less drawings
+	
Profits	Surpluses from previous years

Recording transactions

General ledger

- Contains all individual accounts needed to record business transactions.
- Shows double entry recording of all transactions.

Double entry rules

Debit entries record:	Credit entries record:
↑ in assets	↓ in assets
↓ in liabilities	↑ in liabilities
Expenses	Income
Drawings	Injections of capital

Credit transactions and sales tax

Credit transactions	Sales tax
Credit transaction = goods exchanged before payment made.	Applies to businesses registered for sales tax.
However transactions are recorded as they occur therefore need payable/receivable accounts.	**Sales** • Must add sales tax to sales made • Typical sales tax rate = 20% • Receivable amount recorded gross of sales tax • Sale recorded net of sales tax.
Credit purchase 1 Purchase recorded and payable account set up showing amount due to supplier 2 Amount is later paid from bank.	**Purchases** • Sales tax charged on price by supplier • Payables amount is recorded gross of sales tax • Purchase recorded net of sales tax.

Credit sale
 1 Sale recorded and receivable account setup showing amount due from receivable
 2 Debtor pays invoice.
	Net sales tax
	     Tax on sales X
	     Tax on purchases (X)
	     Tax payables to authorities X

Recording transactions

Purchases and sales tax

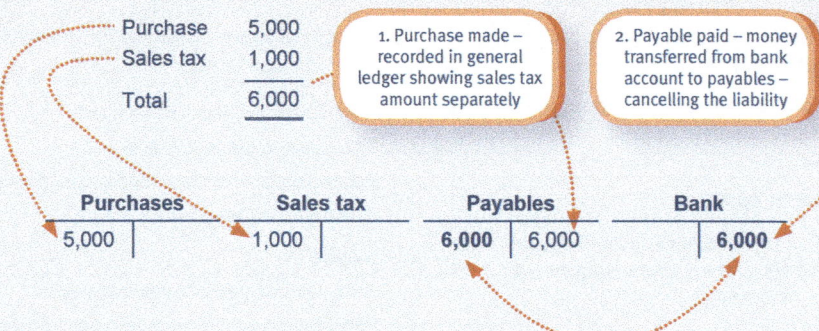

Sales and sales tax

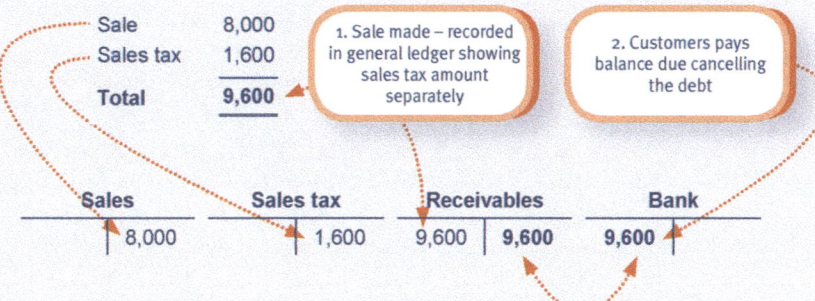

Recording transactions

Net sales tax

- Calculated regularly (e.g. every 1 or 3 months)
- Excess of sales tax charged over incurred is paid to tax authorities

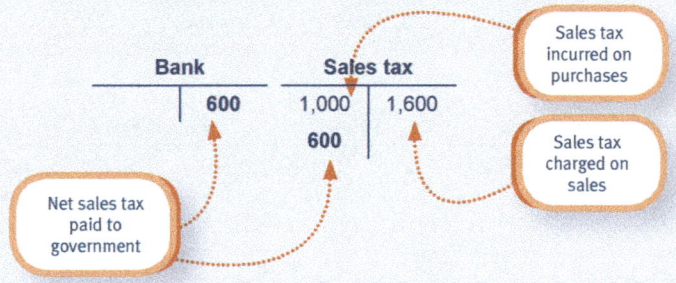

Exam focus

Sales tax is not relevant to all questions. Read the question carefully to decide whether it needs to be considered.

Ledgers – key definitions

> **Definition**

A ledger is a collection of ledger accounts, each account recording transactions of the same type.

- General ledger = holds all individual ledger accounts used to prepare the financial statements.
- Personal ledgers = receivables ledger and payables ledger, holding individual accounts for all receivables/payables.
- Books of original (or prime) entry = books in which transactions are originally recorded:
  - Sales day book (credit sales)
  - Purchase day book (credit purchases)
  - Cash received day book
  - Cheque payments day book
  - Petty cash book
  - Journal.

Recording transactions

Discounts

Discounts

Trade discounts = discount given for ordering in large quantities as an incentive for regular customers

- Reduction in selling price at point of sale
- Record transaction at discounted price

Settlement discounts = discount given for early payment of a debt (within a stated period of time)

Settlement discounts = discount given for early settlement of an amount due i.e. pay supplier within 7 days of invoice date

- Seller to decide at point of sale whether settlement discount terms likely to be taken up by customer
- If probable that settlement discount terms will be taken up by customer, deduct from price in arriving at invoice amount
- If probable that settlement discount terms will not be taken up by customer, do not deduct from price in arriving at invoice amount
- Adjust for any cash received in excess of receivable recorded (or of shortfall of cash received) against revenue

Purchaser decides whether to take advantage of settlement discount terms

If will do so, pay reduced amount and record discount received to clear payable previously recorded as follows:

Dr PLCA
Cr Cash
Cr Discount received

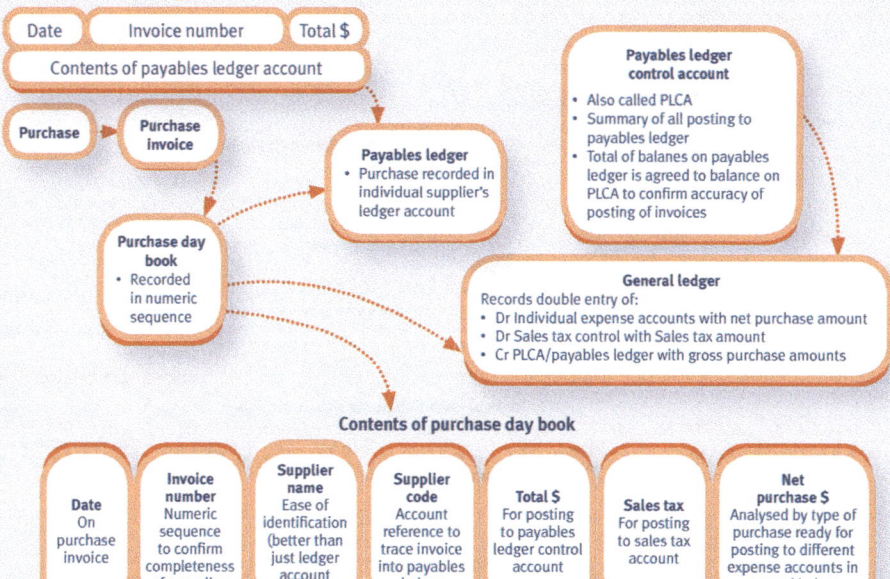

Recording transactions

Cash payments cycle

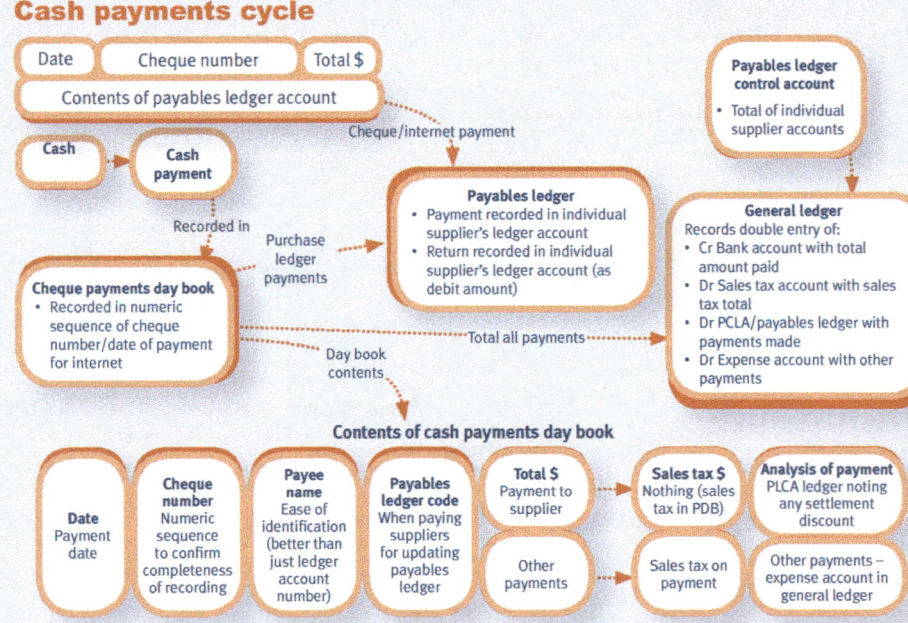

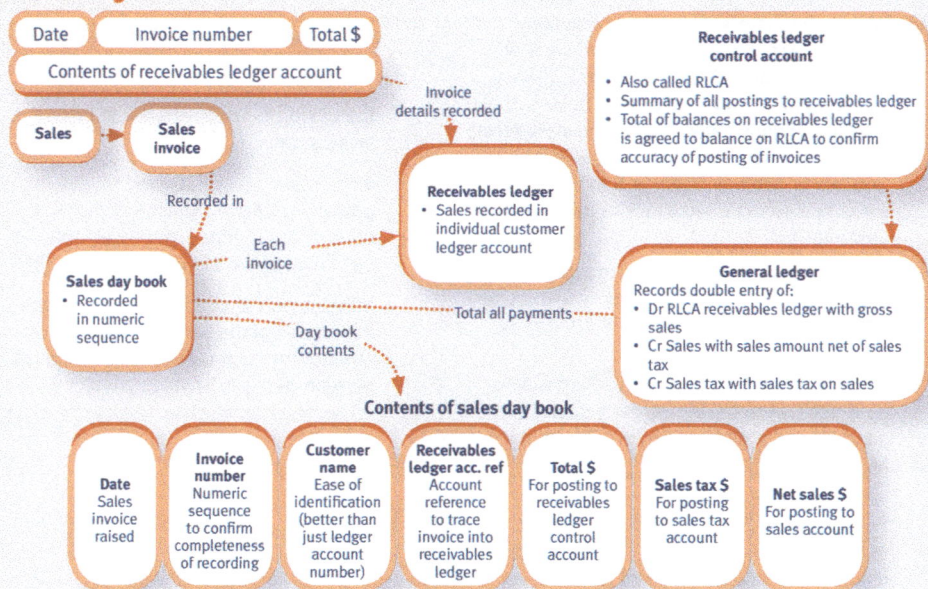

Variable consideration

When goods are sold on credit, the seller must estimate the amount of revenue that will be receivable. Trade discount is always deducted in arriving at the price to be invoiced. If early settlement terms are offered to the customer, the seller must estimate whether or not it is probable that the early settlement terms offered will be taken by the customer.

If it is probable that early settlement will be made by the customer, then early settlement discount should be deducted in arriving at the invoice price.

If it is probable that early settlement will not be made by the customer, early settlement discount is not deducted in arriving at the invoice price.

When cash is subsequently received from the customer, any under- or over-receipt of cash (in comparison with the receivable recorded) is adjusted against revenue.

Example

A business sold goods to a customer on credit at a list price of $240. Early settlement discount of 4% was offered to the customer for payment within 7 days of invoice date.

If the customer is expected to take advantage of the settlement discount offered, the revenue and receivable will be recorded as: $240 × 96% = $230.40.

If the customer is not expected to take advantage of the settlement discount offered, the revenue and receivable will be recorded as $240.

Cash receipts cycle

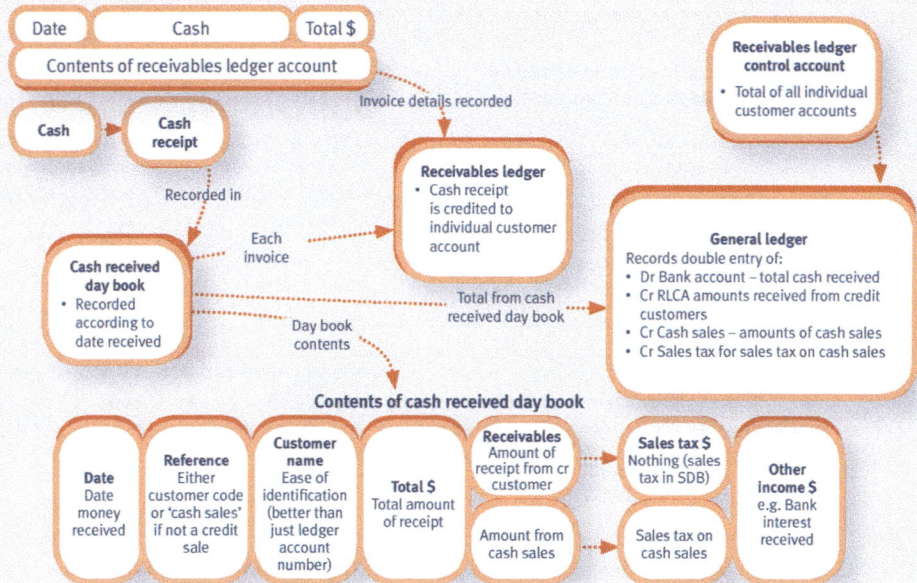

Recording transactions

Journal

Definition

A journal is a record containing details of non-routine double entry transactions.

Uses of journal

- Correction of errors
- Year-end adjustments (e.g. depreciation)
- Recording of significant transactions (e.g. non-current asset purchase).

Exam focus

Many examination questions focus on the double entry required for different accounting transactions. Ensure you can prepare entries as T accounts as well as journals. Even with multiple-choice questions, it can be useful to prepare working T accounts to check the double entry of different transactions.

Format of journal

				31 December 20X4
Reference	Detail	General ledger ref.	Debit $	Credit $
52	Depreciation charge on motor vehicles	GL78	7,800	
	Accum. depreciation on motor vehicles	GL54		7,800
	Year end depreciaition charge for motor vehicles			

Exam focus

If a question asks for a journal, be sure to provide the Dr, Cr and narrative explanation.

Key Point

The receivables and payables ledger control accounts are normally part of the double entry system. The receivables and payables ledgers containing individual customer and supplier accounts are not. You MUST, however, ensure that both are updated with entries in the day books.

Definition

Control accounts are accounts which contain only totals rather than several individual entries. For example, the receivables ledger control account contains totals from the sales day book.

Recording transactions

chapter 2

Trial balance

In this chapter

- Reasons for producing a trial balance.
- Limitations of a trial balance.
- Producing a trial balance.
- Errors not identified by a trial balance.
- Correction of errors not identified by a trial balance.
- Errors identified by a trial balance.
- The suspense account.
- Correction of errors involving a suspense account.

Trial balance

Reasons for producing a trial balance

- Check that double entry procedures have been followed: total debits should = total credits
- Starting point for the preparation of income statement and statement of financial position
- Shows current balances on all accounts – useful for management
- Helps identify errors in accounting records.

Definition

The trial balance is a list of balances extracted from the general ledger.

Limitations of a trial balance

- Only identifies some errors
- Does not identify where errors have been made or what they are.

Producing a trial balance

1. Balance all accounts in general ledger
2. List balances of all accounts separating debit and credit balances as shown on right (some headings e.g. assets will have more than one entry in a 'real' trial balance)
3. Total the debits and credits – they should be the same
4. Where the total debits do not equal the total credits, investigate and find reason(s) for discrepancy.

Balances on a trial balance

Trial balance

	Dr	Cr
Assets	$	
Liabilities		$
Capital		$
Drawings (from capital)	$	
Income (sales)		$
Discounts received		$
Purchase returns		$
Expenses	$	
Sales returns	$	
Irrecoverable debts	$	
Should be the same	**Total**	**Total**

Errors not identified by a trial balance

In all of the following examples, the errors do not result in an imbalance to the trial balance. This is because, even though an error has been made, the debit entry = the credit entry.

Error	Example
Error of commission Correct amount entered into correct category of account but wrong account.	The purchase of a motor vehicle recorded in the premises account.
Error of principle Correct amount entered but in the wrong 'class' of account.	Amount for a motor vehicle repair entered as a debit in the motor vehicle account (treating an expense as an asset addition).
Error of complete omission A transaction has not been recorded at all.	Purchase invoice not entered into the accounts.
Compensating errors One error coincidentally cancelled by another of the same amount.	A cash sale of $30 is accidentally debited to cash as $3 and depreciation of $27 is debited to depreciation expense but not credited to accumulated depreciation.
Original entry errors: debit and credit wrong The debit and credit entries are equal but for the wrong amount.	A cash purchase of $90 is entered into the purchases and cash accounts as $19.
Error of complete reversal The double entry is correct in every respect other than the debit and credit are posted the wrong way round.	Payment of an electricity bill is recorded as a credit to electricity expense and a debit to bank.

Correction of errors not identified by a trial balance

The best approach is to consider:

1. What double entry should have been posted (i.e. what is the correct double entry to record the transaction)? (SHOULD DO)
2. What double entry was posted? (DID DO)
3. What entry is therefore required to move from the entry that was posted to the entry that should have been posted? (TO CORRECT)

Example

A cash purchase of $90 is entered into the purchases and cash accounts as $19.

Should do	Did do	To correct
Dr Purchases $90	Dr Purchases $19	Dr Purchases $71
Cr Cash $90	Cr Cash $19	Cr Cash $71
		To record the purchases previously unrecorded

↑

The correction journal should always have an equal debit and credit.

Trial balance

Errors identified by a trial balance

Errors in producing the trial balance
- An account is balanced incorrectly meaning that the amount shown in the trial balance is wrong
- An account is completely omitted from the trial balance
- A debit balance is placed in the credit column or vice versa.

Errors identified by the trial balance

Error	Example
Error of partial omission Either the debit or credit entry has not been posted to the accounts.	The owner injects capital into the business and the only entry is to debit cash.
Original entry errors: either debit or credit wrong One entry is for the correct amount, but the other is for a different amount.	Rental income of $450 is credited correctly but the debit entry is made for $45.
Transposition error Arises where two numbers within a balance are reversed when entering the transaction into the ledgers. This normally only occurs on one side of the entry. If it occurs on both, the TB will not identify the error.	Drawings of $120 are correctly recorded in the bank ledger but recorded as $210 in the drawings ledger.
Double debit or double credit A transaction is recorded as two debits or two credits.	A cash payment for motor expenses is debited to both the cash and motor expense accounts. No credit entry is made.

The suspense account

Definition

The suspense account is a multi-purpose account used to:

- record entries where the bookkeeper is not sure where the entries should be recorded
- highlight errors in the accounting system which have arisen as a result of the breakdown in double entry (i.e. errors identified by the trial balance).

Key Point

- Where debits ≠ credits in the trial balance, a suspense account is used to make up the difference so that debits do = credits.
- The suspense account requires clearing prior to preparation of the financial statements.

Exam focus

Remember that not all errors involve the suspense account – in an exam question, the majority will probably not.

Correction of errors involving a suspense account

Errors in producing the trial balance

Error	Correction	Example
An account is balanced incorrectly meaning that the amount shown in the trial balance is wrong.	Adjust the amount in the trial balance to be correct and send the opposite entry to the suspense account.	A cash balance of $560 has been wrongly extracted from the general ledger and listed in the trial balance. The balance should be $580. Increase the cash balance in the TB by $20 (a debit) and credit suspense with $20.
An account is completely omitted from the trial balance.	Insert the account in the trial balance and send the opposite entry to the suspense account.	Accruals of $200 have been omitted from the TB. Add the accruals balance to the credit side of the TB and debit suspense with $200.
A debit balance is placed in the credit column or vice versa.	Show the balance in the correct column of the TB and send double the amount of the balance to suspense.	Sales of $23,000 are shown in the debit column of the TB. Move to the credit column (by crediting $46,000) and debit suspense with $46,000.

Chapter 2

Errors identified by the trial balance

- Again the best approach is the 'should do', 'did do', 'to correct' approach.
- When considering 'did do', there will not be an equal debit and credit.
- You may find it helpful to think about the suspense account arising here to make the entries equal.
- The correction journal will then always involve the reversal of any 'did do' suspense entry.
- The correction journal should always include equal debits and credits.

Example

An injection of capital of $450 was recorded correctly in the capital account but as $540 in the bank ledger.

Should do	Did do	To correct
Dr Bank $450	Dr Bank $540	Dr Suspense $90
Cr Capital $450	Cr Capital $450	Cr Bank $90
	(Cr Suspense $90)	To reverse the extra amount debited to bank.

Trial balance

Exam focus

Some of the hardest examination questions involve the clearing of a suspense account balance. Try to follow the procedures outlined above for each error found, being very careful to get the debits and credits of the correcting entry right. Always deal with the easiest corrections first.

chapter 3

Final accounts – introduction and accounting policies

In this chapter

- Preparing the statement of profit or loss/ statement of financial position.
- Format and preparation of accounts.
- Users of accounts.
- Accounting principles.
- Accounting policies.
- Qualitative characteristics of useful financial information.

Final accounts – introduction and accounting policies

Preparing the statement of profit or loss / statement of financial position

Statement of profit or loss	Statement of financial position (balance sheet)
1 Identify revenue and expense accounts in the general ledger.	1 Identify asset and liability accounts in the general ledger.
2 Find balances on individual accounts.	2 Find balances on individual accounts.
3 Transfer balances to income statement.	3 Transfer balances to the statement of financial position.

- Accounts should be prepared regularly as required.
- Prepared annually for filing and taxation purposes.

Definition

Trading account = sales less cost of goods sold to give gross profit.

Exam focus

You must learn the format of the statement of profit or loss and statement of financial position.

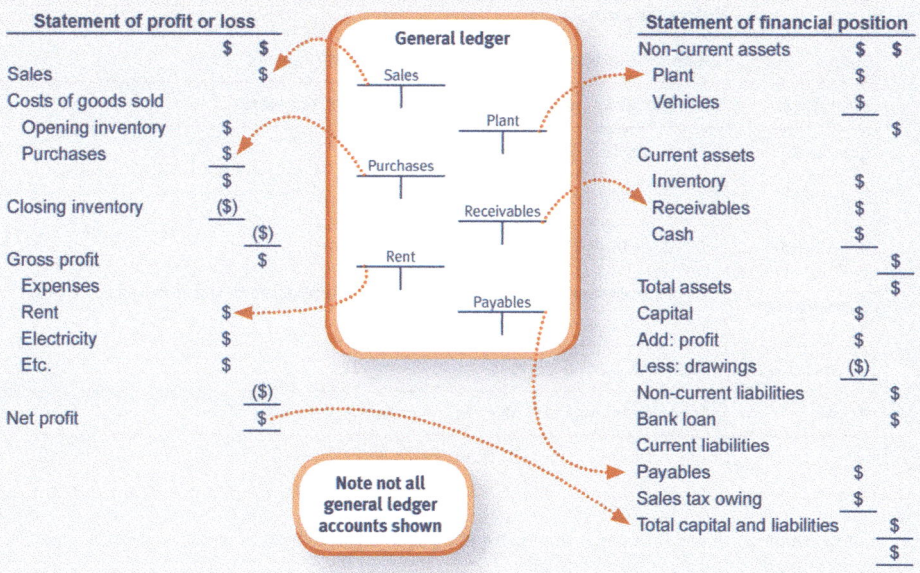

Users of accounts

User	Information needed
Owner	Determine drawings. Improve business performance
Investors	Whether to invest/withdraw capital from the business
Lenders	Check whether loans can be repaid
Suppliers	Ensure entity will pay for goods supplied
Employees	Check company will continue to pay wages
Customers	Ensure business will continue to exist (essential when the business is being relied on e.g. support contracts)
Government	Check tax paid is correct
Public	Monitor business activities (e.g. pressure groups)

Exam focus

If a question asks you to identify why users need financial information, suggest reasons specific to certain users rather than generic to all.

Accounting principles

Business entity
Financial information relates to business only and therefore not to activities of owners

Materiality
A threshold quality – financial statements should separately disclose items that are significant (material) enought to affect users' decisions

Accounting principles

Valuation → **Historic cost**
Values in accounts are based on their historic cost (amount originally entered into the accounts)

Means entity is → **Going concern**
The business will continue in operational existence for the foreseeable future

Accruals
Income recognised when earned – not when cash received
Expenditure recognised when incurred – not when paid for

Conflict → Concepts conflict on income – take realistic view (accruals) but where uncertain prudence wins ← Conflict

Going concern not used → **Break up basis**
Method of accounting used when business will not continue in existence. Assets valued at realisable value – not historic cost less depreciation

Consistency
Similar items treated the same within one accounting period and from one year to the next

Prudence
Use caution under conditions of uncertainty, so that assets or income are not overstated, and liabilities or expenses are not understated

Final accounts – introduction and accounting policies

Accounting policies

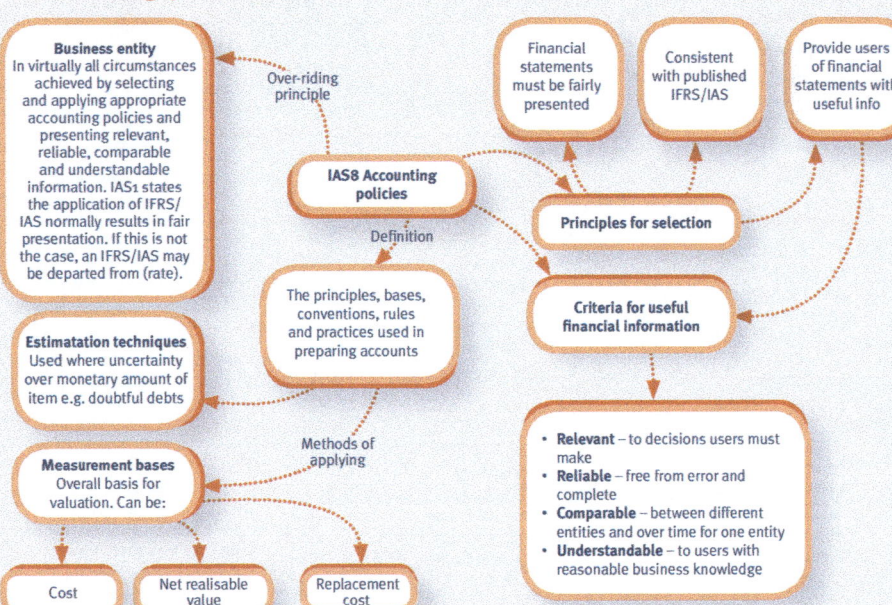

Qualitative characteristics of useful financial information

Two fundamental qualitative characteristics	
Relevance	Information is relevant if it capable of making a difference in the decisions made by users. This is likely to be the case when information can be used to confirm current understanding and/or to or predict future outcomes.
	Materiality is one aspect of relevance - information is material if its omission or misstatement could influence the decisions of users of the financial statements.
Faithful representation	Information should be faithfully represented. This means that accounting information should be presented in accordance with best practice and that the commercial substance of transactions should be presented in the financial statements, rather than their strict legal form. This would imply that such information is complete, neutral or free from bias and free from material error.
Four enhancing qualitative characteristics	
Comparability	Users must be able to compare the financial statements of an enterprise over time to identify trends in its financial position and performance.
	Users must also be able to compare the financial statements of **different enterprises** to evaluate their relative financial positions, performance and financial adaptability.
Verifiability	Information should be capable of either direct verification or indirect verification.
Timeliness	This means that users of information have access to that information within timescales which are appropriate for their decision-making purposes.
Understandability	Information in financial statements must be understandable to its users. This may depend upon how knowledgeable individuals are when evaluating financial information.

Final accounts – introduction and accounting policies

Exam focus

This section has focused on explaining accounting terms – both multiple choice and essay type questions will check your knowledge of these terms.

It is vital that you learn what each one means.

chapter 4

Non-current assets

In this chapter

- Capital and revenue expenditure.
- Non-current assets – key points.
- Accounting for non-current assets.
- Depreciation overview.
- Accounting for depreciation.
- Changes in depreciation.
- Disposals of non-current assets.
- Disposal and part exchange.
- Asset register.
- Asset counts.

Capital and revenue expenditure

Revenue expenditure	Capital expenditure
• Relates to one accounting period. • Is matched against revenue generated in that accounting period. • Example = inventory purchased for resale is matched to the sale of the inventory in the income statement.	• Relates to more than one accounting period. • Is matched against the accounting periods when the capital expenditure generates income by way of depreciation. • Example = a computer with a useful economic life of 3 years is depreciated over 3 years.

Definition

Capital expenditure is expenditure on non-current assets.

Non-current assets – key points

Assets

Current assets
- Assets which will either be converted into cash within the next 12 months, or
- Will be consumed within the entity's normal operating cycle.

Examples: inventory, receivables, cash

Non-current assets
Assets which are purchased for continuing use within the business in the generation of profits over more than one accounting period.

Tangible non-current assets
Assets which can be physically touched, e.g. property, machines, vehicles.

Statement of financial position presentation
Typically grouped into categories, e.g.:
- Land and buildings
- Fixtures and fittings
- Motor vehicles.

Exam focus

Non-current assets are very examinable within multiple choice, short-form and longer questions. You must get to grips with this chapter.

Non-current assets

Accounting for non-current assets

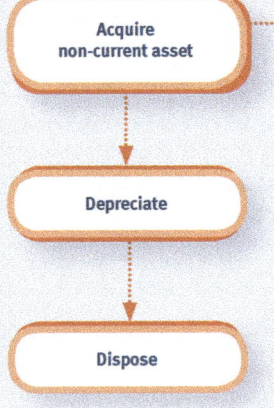

Record at cost:
- Dr Non-current asset
- Cr Cash / payables

Cost includes all costs directly attributable to bringing the asset to the location and condition necessary for use:
- Purchase price of asset
- Delivery costs
- Site preparation
- Installation and assembly
- Associated professional fees

Sales tax is generally recoverable:
- Dr Non-current asset   net cost
- Dr Sales tax account   sales tax
- Cr Cash / payable   gross cost

Sales tax on motor vehicles may not be recoverable. Therefore it becomes part of the cost of the asset.

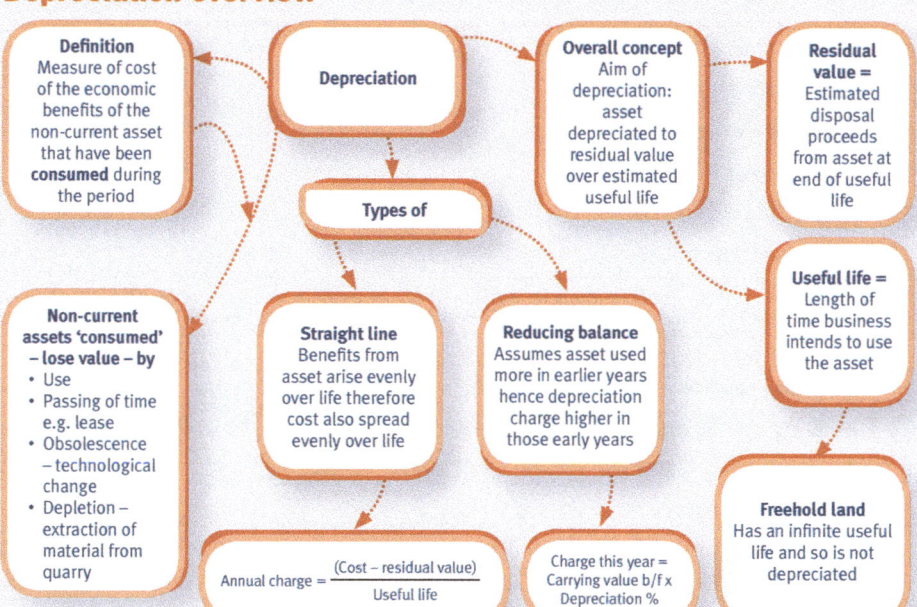

Non-current assets

Example

Straight line

Asset cost = $9,000

Useful life = 6 years

Residual value = $3,000

Depreciation = $1,000 pa

= (9,000-3,000) / 6 years

Example

Reducing balance

Asset CV b/f = $6,000

Depreciation rate = 25% pa

Depreciation = 6,000 x 25% = $1,500

CV c/f = $4,500

Accounting for depreciation

Accounting options

Charge a full year's depreciation in year of purchase, then none in year of sale.

Charge depreciation for each month the asset is used by the entity (pro-rata depreciation).

Accounting entries

Basic accounting entry is:

Dr Depreciation expense
(statement of profit or loss)

Cr Accumulated depreciation
(statement of financial position)

Depreciation double entry:

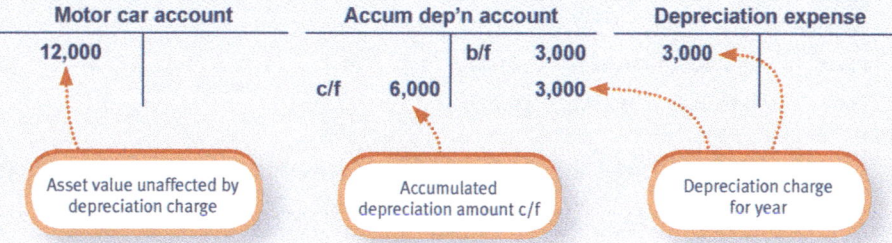

Asset value therefore:

Cost − Accumulated depreciation = Carrying value (CV)

12,000 − 6,000 = 6,000

Non-current assets

Exam focus

Note the accumulated depreciation account is also called the provision for depreciation account in some texts / questions.

Financial statements presentation

	Cost	Accum dep,n	CV
Motor vehicles	12,000	(6,000)	6,000
Plant	32,000	(18,000)	14,000
Total	44,000	(24,000)	20,000

- Cost, accumulated depreciation and carrying value for each class of non-current asset are given either on the face of the statement of financial position (balance sheet) or in a note to the accounts.
- A single depreciation expense account is listed in the statement of profit or loss.

Changes in depreciation

Change in useful life

- Write off remaining CV over remaining useful life.

Change in method of depreciation

- Only change if the new method will show a fairer presentation in the accounts.
- If change, write off the carrying value over the remaining useful life using the new method.

Disposals of non-current assets

1. Transfer cost to disposals account.
2. Transfer accumulated depreciation to disposals account.
3. Enter sale proceeds into cash book and disposals account.
4. Find balance on disposals account.
   - Profit = Dr Disposals / Cr Statement of profit or loss
   - Loss = Dr Statement of profit or loss / Cr Disposals.

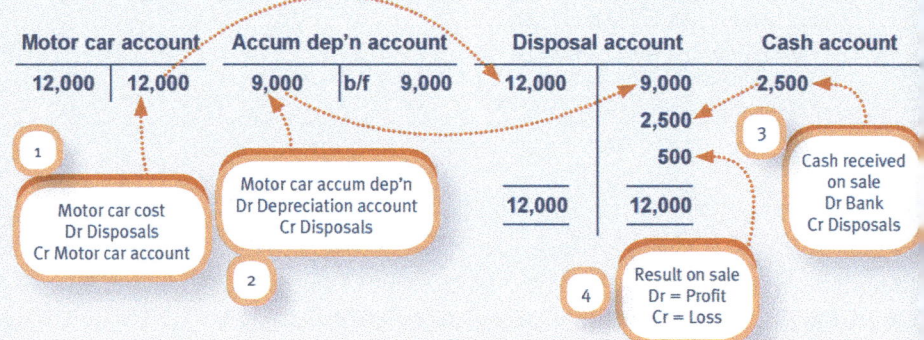

Key Point

If a non-current asset is 'scrapped', disposal proceeds are nil.

Disposal and part exchange

Situation where old asset is sold in part payment for new asset.

1. Transfer cost to disposals account (as disposal above – not shown on diagram below).

2. Transfer accumulated depreciation to disposals account (as disposal above – not shown on diagram below).

3. Enter purchase of new motor car as Dr Asset account (with full value) and Cr Cash book (with amount paid) and Cr Disposal account (with part exchange proceeds).

4. Find balance on disposals account
   - Profit = Dr Disposals / Cr Statement of profit or loss
   - Loss = Dr Statement of profit or loss / Cr Disposals.

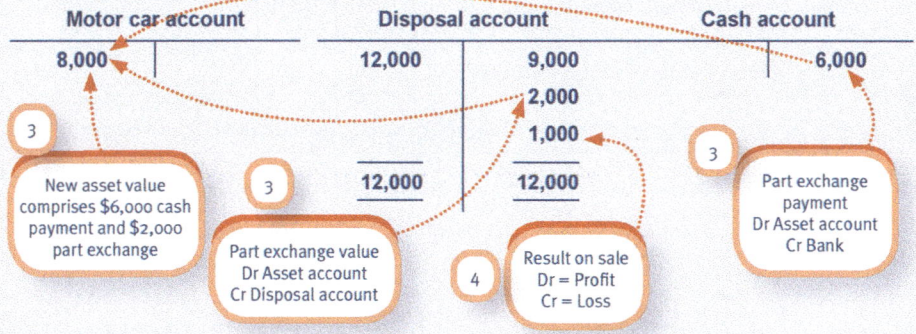

Non-current assets

Exam focus

Many examination questions focus on calculation of depreciation and the profit/loss on sale. Ensure you are happy with the double entry for these calculations.

Asset register

Definition

A collection of records, one for each asset, carrying detailed information about each asset.

Example of information contained in register:

Asset number	Description	Location	Supplier ref	Useful life	Dep'n method	Cost $	Scrap value $	Accum Dep'n b/f $	CV $	Date of disposal	Disposal proceeds $

Non-current asset register should be agreed to the general ledger monthly/annually. Acts as a control over completeness of the general ledger.

Non-current assets

Asset counts

Definition

The inspection of assets owned by the business to check the accuracy and validity of entries in the asset register.

Procedure	Procedure for errors
1 List assets from the asset register. 2 Locate each asset – check against list – and determine condition. 3 Mark asset as counted (e.g. attach a coloured sticker). 4 Identify assets not marked as counted. 5 Identify any missing items from list.	**Non-current asset missing** • Remove asset from the asset register. **Non-current assets not in register** • Add to register – but at zero cost. • Likely that the asset was mis-categorised as revenue expenditure in the past.

chapter 5

Control account reconciliations

In this chapter

- Purpose of control accounts.
- Control account reconciliation.
- Summary of errors and corrections required.
- Suppliers' statements.
- Effect of errors on profit and net assets.

Control account reconciliations

Purpose of control accounts

Receivables ledger control account
Provides the receivables balance at any given time

Should equal total of personal accounts in sales ledger

Receivables ledger
Includes personal accounts for each credit customer

←···· Normally part of double entry ····→

Payables ledger control account
Provides the payables balance at any given time

Should equal total of personal accounts in purchase ledger

Payables ledger
Includes personal accounts for each credit supplier

←···· Not normally part of double entry ····→

Control accounts:

- Provide total receivables/payables for the balance sheet.
- Act as a control over the sales and purchase ledgers.
- Can assist in the calculation of missing figures where records are incomplete.

Exam focus

A common question in the exam is to give reasons for using control accounts. Ensure you are specific in your answer and consider whether the question refers to a particular type of control account.

Update of RLCA and individual ledger

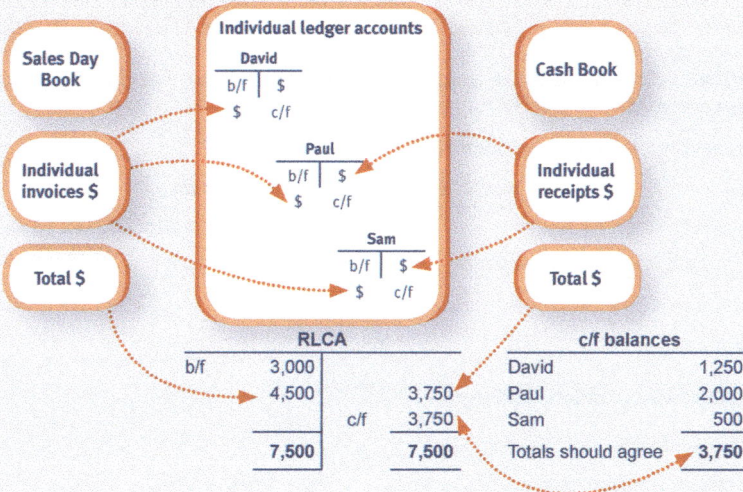

- Note c/f balances are obtained from each individual ledger account.
- These agree in total to the total carried forward on the RLCA.

Control account reconciliation

Definition

A control account reconciliation is an exercise carried out to ensure that the control account balances agree with the totals in the personal ledgers.

Proforma control account reconciliation – receivables ledger

Receivables ledger control account

Balance b/f	X	Corrections to control account errors	X
Corrections to control account errors	X	Revised balance c/f	Y
	X		X
Revised balance b/f	Y		

Receivables ledger reconciliation

Total list of balances originally extracted	X
Corrections to errors in personal accounts	X/(X)
Adjusted list of balances	Y

Error	Effect	To correct...
SDB undercast by $300	Posting to sales account and RLCA $300 short	Dr RLCA $300 Cr Sales $300
Invoice in PDB for $890 recorded in personal account as $980	Purchases and PLCA correct – only individual ledger account affected	Dr Personal account $90 (reduces balance on personal account)
Cash receipt from Sam entered as Dr $500 in Sam's individual ledger account	SLCA correct – Sam's account balance $1,000 overstated (double posting error)	Cr Sam's account $1,000
Discount received column in cash book for $80 not totalled or posted to general ledger	PLCA and discounts received account both understated by $80	Dr PLCA $80 Cr Discounts rec'd $80
Balance of $750 owing from Peter omitted from purchase ledger list of balances	Total PLCA does not agree to list of balances – however all double-entry bookkeeping correct	Include Peter's balance in list of balances
Credit balance on Smith's account for $120 in sales ledger added as debit balance in list of balances	Double entry bookkeeping OK – list of balances overstated by double amount of balance	Reduce the total of list of balances by $240

Control account reconciliations

Summary of errors and corrections required

Error	Correction required in Control account	Correction required in Personal ledger
Incorrect column addition in day book	Yes	No
Incorrect entry/omission of transaction in day book	Yes	Yes
Incorrect/omission of transfer of total from day book	Yes	No
Incorrect/omission of transfer of individual transaction from day book	No	Yes
Incorrect extraction/omission of personal account balance from list of balances	No	No (amend list of balances only)
Incorrect addition/balancing of personal account	No	Yes

Exam focus

Reconciliations are tested very regularly. You must ensure that:

- you show amendments to the ledger account as debits or credits rather than additions or deductions to the existing balance
- you do not confuse the draft balance for the ledger account with the draft total of individual balances
- you check whether the draft balance on the ledger account is a debit or a credit
- you balance off the ledger account and total the reconciliation.

Suppliers' statements

- = monthly statement often sent by suppliers which lists movements on the account
- A suppliers' statement reconciliation can then be performed as an additional check.

Effect of errors on profit and net assets

The effect can easily be determined by reference to the correction journal:

Correction journal	Impact on profit	Impact on net assets
Dr Statement of financial position account Cr Profit or loss account	Increase	Increase
Dr Profit or loss account Cr Statement of financial position account	Decrease	Decrease
Dr Profit or loss account Cr Profit or loss account	No impact	No impact
Dr Statement of financial position account Cr Statement of financial position account	No impact	No impact

NB for the purpose of this exercise, a suspense account = statement of financial position item.

Exam focus

The impact of correction journals may be required as part of a reconciliation or suspense account question. The easiest approach is to set up an adjustments to profit/net assets working and deal with each adjustment as you come to it in the process of producing the reconciliation/clearing the suspense account.

chapter 6

Bank reconciliation

In this chapter

- Need for a bank reconciliation.
- Reasons for differences.
- Dishonoured cheques.
- Format of bank reconciliation.
- Preparing a bank reconciliation.
- Petty cash.
- The imprest system.

Bank reconciliation

Need for a bank reconciliation

A bank reconciliation:

- Checks the accuracy of the cash account by agreeing the balance to an independent source
- Identifies errors (in the cash account and made by the bank)
- Explains the difference between the balance on the cash account and the balance on the bank statement.

Reasons for differences

Reasons for differences

Items on bank statement but not in cash book (unrecorded differences)

Items that the business does not know about until the bank statement arrives:

- Bank charges
- Bank interest
- Direct debits/credits
- Dishonoured cheques
- Standing order

Items in cash book but not in bank statement (timing differences)

Unpresented (uncleared) cheques =

cheques written by the business but either not yet paid in or not yet cleared by the bank

Outstanding (uncleared) deposits =

amounts paid into the bank by the business which have not yet gone through the bank's clearing system

Dishonoured cheques

Definition

Dishonoured cheques are cheques that the drawer's bank refuses to honour – normally because the drawer's bank account is overdrawn.

Customer therefore still owes amount due.

Double entry for returned cheque is:

Dr   RLCA (and receivable's personal account in the receivables ledger)

   Cr Bank

Bank reconciliation

Format of bank reconciliation

Cash ledger account

Balance b/d	X		
Bank interest (received)	X	Bank interest (paid)	X
Direct credit	X	Direct debit	X
		Bank charges	X
		Standing order	X
		Dishonoured cheques	X
		Balance c/d	X
	X		X
Balance b/d	Y		

Bank reconciliation	$
Balance on the bank statement	X
Less: unpresented cheques	(X)
Add: outstanding deposits	X
Revised bank balance	Y

Preparing a bank reconciliation

1. Set out a proforma cash account and bank reconciliation.

2. Tick the bank statement to the day books. Update for items included in the bank statement but not entered in the day books. In the exam this is achieved by making adjustments directly to the cash account.

3. Tick the cash received and cheque payments day books to the bank statement to identify unpresented cheques and outstanding deposits. Adjust for these in the bank reconciliation proforma.

4. Balance the cash account and agree the balance to the completed bank reconciliation.

5. The revised balance is shown in the statement of financial position.

Exam focus

Bank reconciliation questions tend to include similar adjustments. Make sure you are familiar with them. Deal with these common adjustments first in a bank reconciliation question and leave any trickier points until later.

Bank reconciliation

Petty cash

Definition

Petty cash is money held on business premises to meet everyday expenses.

Money taken out of petty cash to pay expenses and replaced with voucher (X):

Dr Profit or loss expense
Dr Sales tax
Cr Petty cash

Recording of petty cash

Contents of petty cash book						
Date	Details	Voucher reference	Total $	Sales tax $	Travel $	Other expenses $
			X X X ― A			

Balance b/d
Less total expenses
Add cash replenishments
Balance c/d

Required float
(A)
A
Required float

Cash from bank to reimburse petty cash balance (A):

Dr Petty cash
Cr Bank

The imprest system

Definition

An imprest system is one where, at any point in time, the sum of the cash held and the values of the vouchers raised in the period will equal a predetermined amount (the float or imprest amount).

- Float is set at a level thought sufficient to cover everyday expenses over a period (e.g. one week).
- Money taken out of petty cash for purchases is replaced by an authorised voucher detailing the transaction and attached to a receipt.

At any point in time:

CASH + VOUCHERS = FLOAT

If not, this may be due to:

- voucher made out wrongly and ≠ cash paid out
- cash stolen
- wrong amount of cash paid out
- At regular intervals, the vouchers are removed and totalled and an equal amount is withdrawn from the bank to replenish the float.

Bank reconciliation

chapter 7

Accruals, prepayments and irrecoverable debts

In this chapter

- Accruals.
- Prepayments.
- Deferred income.
- Income received in arrears.
- Irrecoverable debts and allowance for receivables – summary.
- Irrecoverable debts – accounting treatment.
- Statement of financial position presentation.

Accruals

An accrual is an item of expense that has been incurred during the accounting period but not paid at the end of that accounting period.

Double entry for accrual is:

- Dr Expense account (in this case rent account)
  - Cr Accruals account on statement of financial position

Determine the amount of accrual as follows:

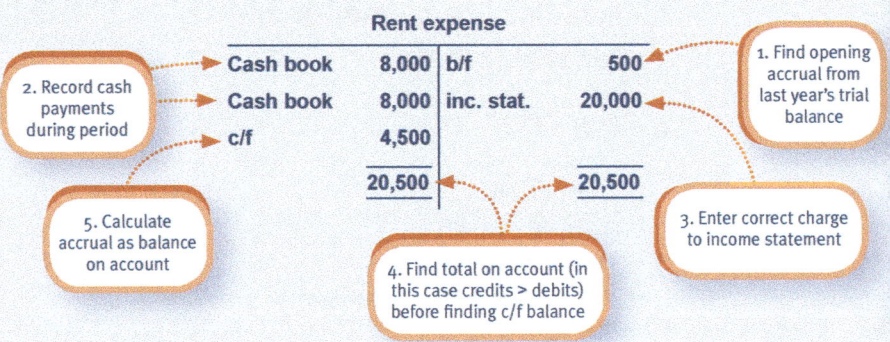

Rent expense

Cash book	8,000	b/f	500
Cash book	8,000	inc. stat.	20,000
c/f	4,500		
	20,500		20,500

1. Find opening accrual from last year's trial balance
2. Record cash payments during period
3. Enter correct charge to income statement
4. Find total on account (in this case credits > debits) before finding c/f balance
5. Calculate accrual as balance on account

Steps 3 and 5 may be reversed depending on the question: you may be given (or be able to calculate) the c/f accrual and so find the statement of profit or loss charge as a balancing figure.

Prepayments

Definition

A prepayment is an item of expense which has been paid during the current accounting period but will not be incurred until the next accounting period.

Determine amount of prepayment as follows:

Double entry for the prepayment is:

- Dr Prepayment account (on statement of financial position)
  - Cr Expense account (in this case insurance)

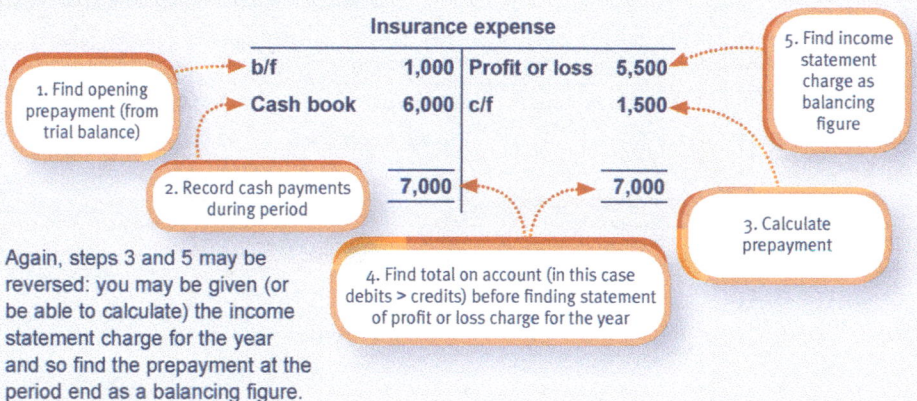

Insurance expense

b/f	1,000	Profit or loss	5,500
Cash book	6,000	c/f	1,500
	7,000		7,000

1. Find opening prepayment (from trial balance)
2. Record cash payments during period
3. Calculate prepayment
4. Find total on account (in this case debits > credits) before finding statement of profit or loss charge for the year
5. Find income statement charge as balancing figure

Again, steps 3 and 5 may be reversed: you may be given (or be able to calculate) the income statement charge for the year and so find the prepayment at the period end as a balancing figure.

Deferred income

Definition

Deferred income is income received in advance.

Accounting treatment is the opposite of expenses payable – as shown below:

Double entry for the rent received in advance is:

Dr Income account (in this case rent receivable)
    Cr Deferred income account (a liability on the statement of financial position)

Note this is a liability because it is an amount owed by the business at the end of the year.

Rental income

Profit or loss	12,000	b/f	1,000
c/f	1,000	Cash book	12,000
	13,000		13,000

1. Find opening deferred income from last year's trial balance
2. Record cash receipts during period
3. Enter statement of profit or loss rent receivable for the period
4. Find total on account (in this case credits > debits) before finding c/f balance
5. Calculate deferred income c/f

Income received in arrears

If income is received in arrears, it is received after the service it relates to is provided. This results in a period-end statement of financial position asset of income owed to the business.

The double entry for the income received in arrears is:

Dr Income due (or accrued income) account (on the statement of financial position)
 Cr Income account (statement of profit or loss)

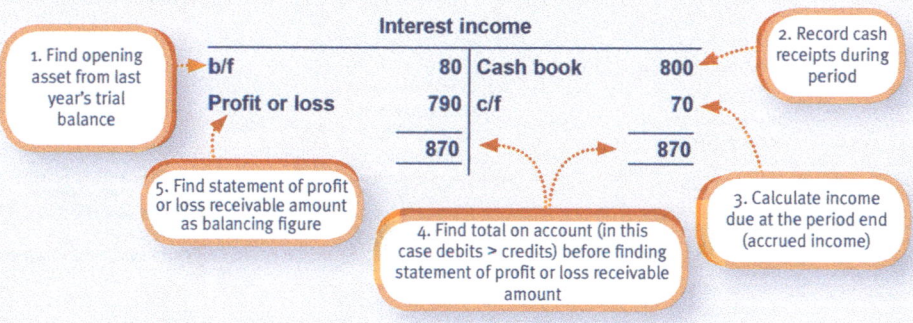

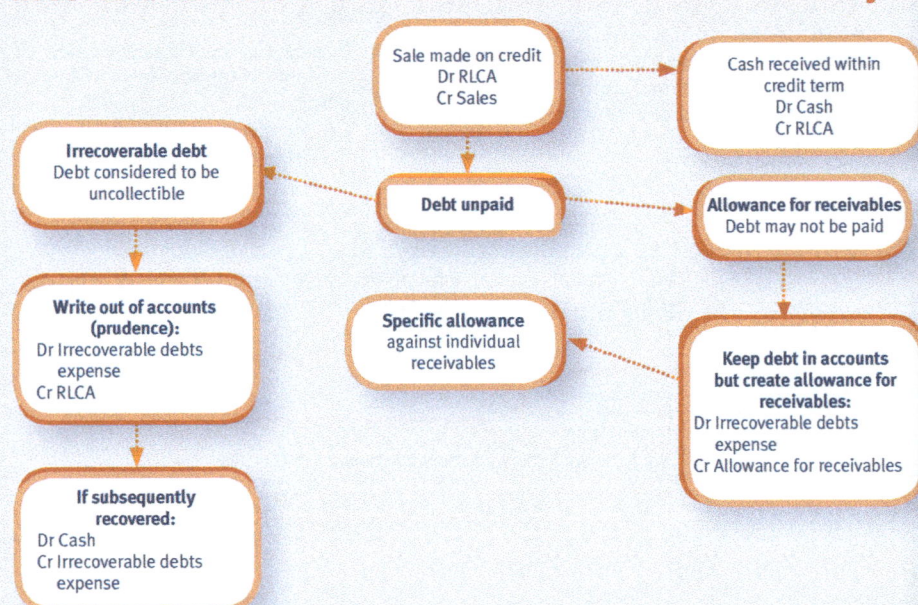

Irrecoverable debts – accounting treatment

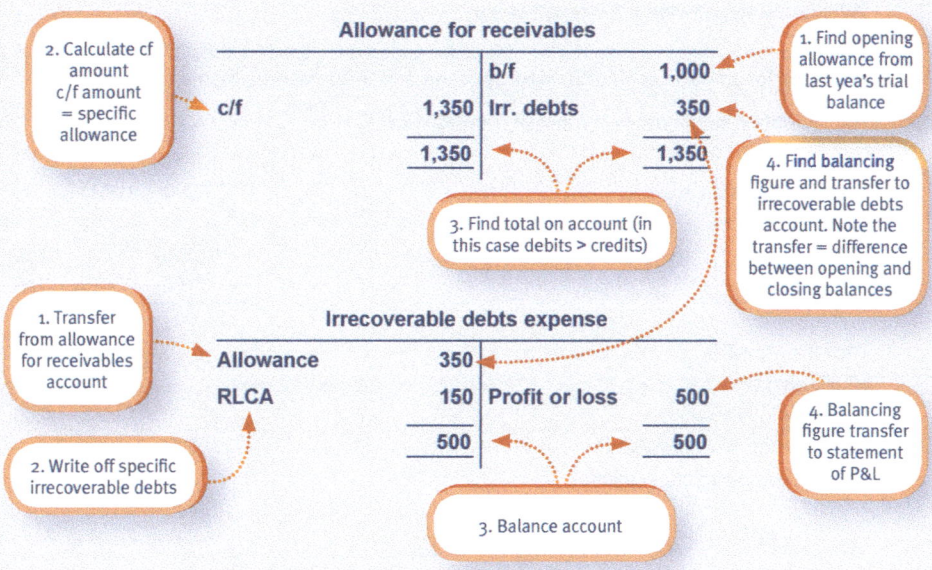

Accruals, prepayments and irrecoverable debts

Example

Calculation of allowance for receivables

Smith's receivables allowance is $23,000 at the period end. Smith wishes to make a specific allowance for amounts of $1,200 owed by Jones and $700 owed by Morgan.

The allowance at the end of the last period was $2,100.

	$	$
Receivables balance	23,000	
Specific allowance		
Jones	(1,200)	1,200
Morgan	(700)	700
	21,000 =	
Total allowance		1,900
b/f allowance		(2,100)
Decrease in allowance		200
Dr Allowance for receivables	200	
Cr Irrecoverable debts expense	200	

Statement of financial position presentation

Prepayment	Shown under current assets
Accrual	Shown under current liabilities
Deferred income	Shown under current liabilities
Income received in arrears	Shown under current assets
Allowance for receivables	Deduct from receivables on statement of financial position
Irrecoverable debts expense	Shown in statement of profit or loss

Exam focus

The two most complicated sections in this chapter are deferred income and the treatment of the allowance for receivables account. Examination questions often ask you to complete these accounts – remember to concentrate on the easier parts of the workings first.

Accruals, prepayments and irrecoverable debts

chapter 8

Closing inventory, liabilities and provisions

In this chapter

- Valuation of inventory.
- Cost v NRV.
- Inventory valuation methods.
- Accounting for inventory.
- Liabilities and provisions.

Closing inventory, liabilities and provisions

Valuation of inventory

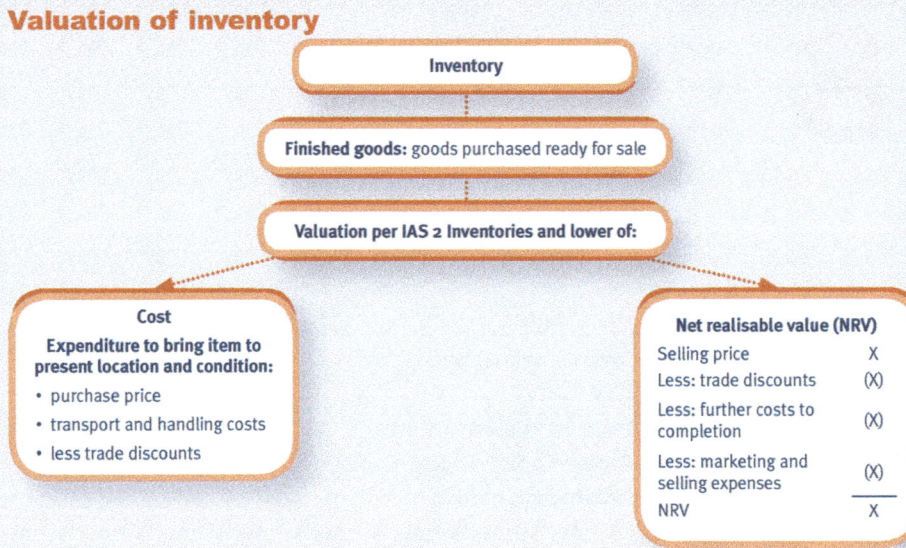

Inventory

Finished goods: goods purchased ready for sale

Valuation per IAS 2 Inventories and lower of:

Cost
Expenditure to bring item to present location and condition:
- purchase price
- transport and handling costs
- less trade discounts

Net realisable value (NRV)

Selling price	X
Less: trade discounts	(X)
Less: further costs to completion	(X)
Less: marketing and selling expenses	(X)
NRV	X

Key Point

When applying the cost v NRV rule to inventories, each line of goods should be considered individually. Some lines will therefore be valued at cost and others at NRV.

Cost v NRV

Valuation options are:

Inventory item	Cost	Selling price	Costs to achieve sale	NRV	Inventory value
A	$2,000	$3,500	nil	$3,500	$2,000
B	$500	$600	$110	$490	$490
C	$1,500	$2,500	$800	$1,700	$1,500
D	$1,000	$1,500	$600	$900	$900

Exam focus

The examiner frequently states in his examiner's reports that students do not know the components of cost and NRV. You MUST learn these and be ready to apply them.

Inventory valuation methods

- Identical products often purchased at different times at different costs → in order to value inventory need to make assumption as to how goods move.
- Method must give good approximation of true cost of inventory.

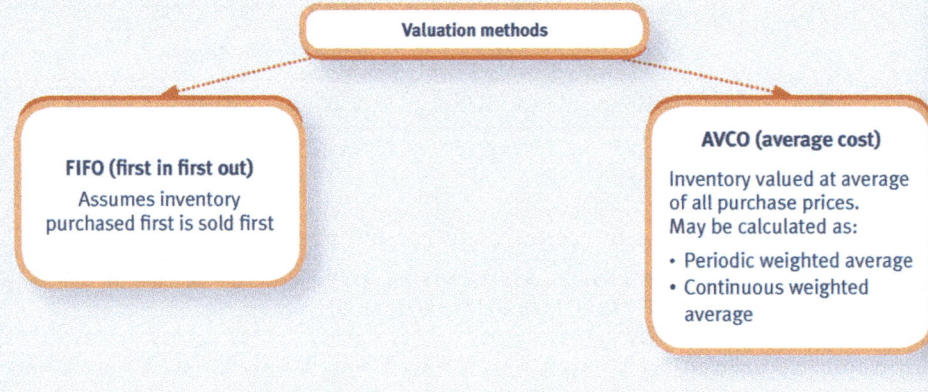

Valuation methods

FIFO (first in first out)
Assumes inventory purchased first is sold first

AVCO (average cost)
Inventory valued at average of all purchase prices.
May be calculated as:
- Periodic weighted average
- Continuous weighted average

Example

		Units	$/unit
1 June	Purchases	100	5
3 June	Sale	10	
4 June	Purchases	200	6
5 June	Sale	170	

FIFO

Purchases	300	units
Sales	(180)	units
Closing inventory	120	units

The 120 units of closing inventory are assumed to be part of the 4th June purchase.

120 units @ $6 = $720

AVCO – periodic weighted average

This method does not consider dates of purchase and sale, instead assuming that all transactions are completed on the last day of the period.

Purchases	$
100 units @ $5	500
200 units @ $6	1,200
300 units	1,700

Closing inventory:

120 units @ $5.67 = $680

Average $1,700/300 units = $5.67

Closing inventory, liabilities and provisions

AVCO – continuous weighted average

This method does consider dates of purchase and sale, with the average price updated after each transaction.

		Units	$/unit	Value
1 June	Purchase	100	5	500
3 June	Sale	(10)	5	(50)
		90		450
4 June	Purchase	200	6	1,200
		290		1,650
5 June	Sale	(170)	$1,650/290 = $5.69	(967)
Closing inventory		120		683

Chapter 8

Accounting for inventory

- During year, inventory purchases always Dr Purchases Cr PLCA
- At end of year, adjustments take place as below

Statement of financial position 31.12.X1 (Extract)			Statement of profit or loss 31.12.X2			Statement of financial position 31.12.X2 (Extract)		
	$	$		$	$		$	$
Non-current assets			Sales		$	Non-current assets		
Plants	$		Cost of goods sold			Plant	$	
Vehicles	$		Opening inventory	$		Vehicle	$	
		$	Purchases	$				$
Current assets				$		Current assets		
Inventory	$		Closing inventory	$		Inventory	$	
Receivables	$				$	Receivables	$	
Cash	$		Gross profit		$	Cash	$	

Double-entry – Opening inventory		Double-entry – Closing inventory	
Dr Opening inventory in statement of profit or loss	$	Dr Inventory statement of financial position	$

Closing inventory, liabilities and provisions

Liabilities and provisions

	Definition	
Liability — An obligation to transfer economic benefits as a result of past transactions or events		**Provision** — A liability of uncertain timing or amount
Dr Purchases / Cr PLCA with credit purchase **or** Dr Bank / Cr Loan account with non-current loan	**Accounting treatment**	Dr Expense account / Cr Provisions (on statement of financial position)
As soon as liability incurred e.g. inventory purchased or loan received from bank	**Recognised**	ONLY recognised when: • Entity has presented obligation (legal or constructive) in response to past event • Probable that transfer of economic benefits needed to settle obligation and • Reliable estimate can be made of amount
	Measures	• At best estimate • Using expected values (example on next page)
Payables: Shown under current liabilities. Loan: Shown under current/non-current liabilities	**Statement of financial position presentation**	Long-term: Shown under non-current liabilities as provisions: Short term: shown under current liabilities under Provisions

- **Legal obligation** = an obligation that is the result of a contract or legislation or other operation of law.
- **Constructive obligation** = an obligation that arises because an entity has indicated, and so created and expectation, that will meet obligations not legally required of it.

Chapter 8

Exam focus

Questions on these areas tend to focus on the different methods of inventory valuation and the accounting treatment of liabilities and provisions – good areas therefore to revise.

Key Point

If part of a loan is due for repayment within a year, it is a current liability. The balance is a non-current liability.

Example

Measurement of provision using expected values

A business provides one-year warranties for the washing machines that it manufactures and sells. There is an 80% chance that no repairs will be needed to a washing machine within the first year; a 15% chance that minor repairs will be needed and a 5% chance that major repairs will be needed. If all machines required minor repairs the cost would be $100,000. If all machines required major repairs the cost would be $200,000. What provision should be made?

Solution

		$
Expected cost of minor repairs	15% x $100,000	15,000
Expected cost of major repairs	5% x $200,000	10,000
Provision required		25,000

Closing inventory, liabilities and provisions

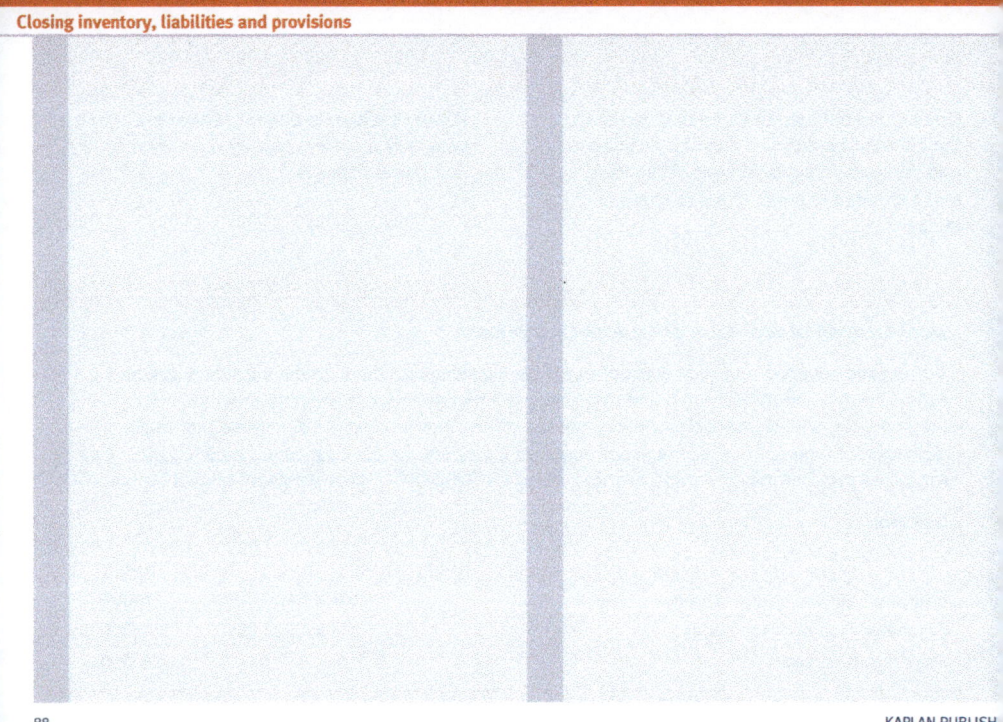

chapter

Extended trial balance

In this chapter

- Preparation summary.
- Format of extended trial balance (ETB).
- ETB and year-end adjustments.
- Completing the ETB.
- Procedure for completion.

Extended trial balance

Preparation summary

- Account balances from the trial balance
- Adjusted for year-end adjustments such as irrecoverable debt write off
- Adjusted for accruals and prepayments
- Cross-cast to produce statement of profit or loss and statement of financial position figures for the year

Chapter 9

Format of extended trial balance (ETB)

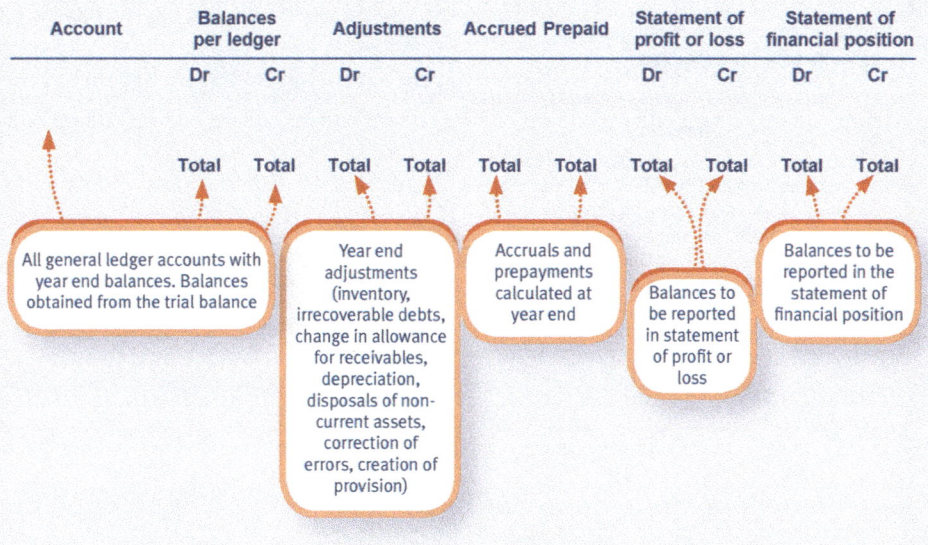

ETB and year-end adjustments

Note list of accounts is not complete – extracts only for examples.

Inventory

Opening inventory placed on Dr of profit and loss account from TB Closing inventory is Dr Statement of financial position and Cr Statement of profit or loss

Completing the ETB

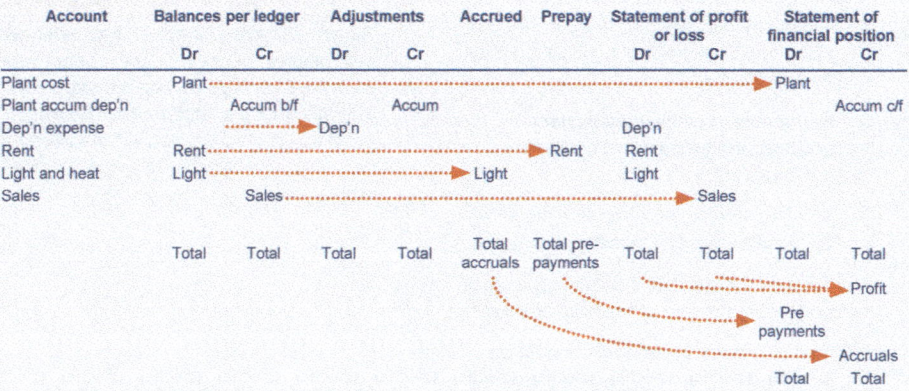

- The rent prepayment is deducted from the rent expense per the ledger when adding across.
- The light and heat accrual is added to the light and heat expense per the ledger when adding across.

Extended trial balance

Procedure for completion

1. Cross-cast all rows and place on Income statement/Statement of financial position as appropriate.

2. Remember to include adjustment, accruals and prepayment columns in cross casting.

3. Total the accruals column and place on Cr of statement of financial position.

4. Total the prepayments column and place on Dr of statement of financial position.

5. Find difference between Dr and Cr on income statement and take to statement of financial position (Dr > Cr = loss; place on Dr of statement of financial position) (Cr > Dr = profit; place on Cr of statement of financial position).

6. Add up statement of financial position columns – should balance!

Exam focus

Remember when completing an extended trial balance you need to think about where each balance is placed on the statement of profit or loss or statement of financial position. In practice, you will also need to cast each row carefully to avoid addition errors.

chapter

10

Sole trader accounts

In this chapter

- Preparation of final accounts.
- Common year-end adjustments.
- Closing the books.

Preparation of final accounts

Final accounts may be prepared from a trial balance or an extended trial balance (as seen in the last chapter).

Preparation from a trial balance

You will be provided with a trial balance and list of year-end adjustments. You should:

1 Work out the double entries for the adjustments.

2 Work out the effect of these entries on the balances in the TB.

3 Slot the adjusted balances into the statement of financial position and statement of profit or loss.

The following pages summarise the common year-end adjustments.

Exam focus

In your exam you should set up the relevant statement of financial position or statement of profit or loss proforma first and then slot in the numbers from the TB. Make any required adjustments to the numbers from the TB in bracketed workings on the face of your proforma statement. Remember to deal with the easiest adjustments first.

Common year-end adjustments

1 Opening and closing inventory

Opening inventory (per TB) is $7,650. Closing inventory is $8,490.

Opening inventory (P&L)			
2 From SOFP	7,650		

Inventory (SFP)			
1 per TB	7,650	2 Trading account balance	7,650
3 Closing inventory	8,490	Bal c/f	8,490
	16,140		16,140
Bal b/f	8,490		

Closing inventory (P&L)			
	8,490	3 Closing inventory	8,490

Sole trader accounts

1. Opening balance of $7,650 is b/d on the statement of financial position inventory account.

2. The opening balance is transferred out of the statement of financial position to the opening inventory account in the statement of profit or loss.

	Dr	Cr
Dr Opening inventory (P&L)	7,650	
Cr Inventory (SFP)		7,650

3. Closing inventory is recorded in both the statement of financial position and statement of profit or loss.

	Dr	Cr
Dr Inventory (SFP)	8,490	
Cr Closing inventory (P&L)		8,490

2 Non-current asset disposals

Van disposed of. Trade in value (part exchange value) $1,000 and cost of new van $3,200. Cost of old van, $2,100; accumulated depreciation $1,000.

Van (cost) account

Old van	2,100	1 Disposals	2,100
3 New van – cash	2,200	Balance c/f	3,200
3 P/E value	1,000		
	5,300		**5,300**
Balance b/f	3,200		

Old van disposal account

1 Van cost	2,100	2 Accum dept	1,000
		3 P/E value	1,000
		4 Loss	100
	2,100		**2,100**

Old van accumulated depreciation

2 Disposals	1,000	2 Depreciation b/f	1,000

Sole trader accounts

		Dr	Cr
1	Transfer cost of original van to disposal account		
	Dr Disposals with old van cost	2,100	
	Cr Van account with old van cost		2,100
2	Transfer accumulated depreciation on original van to disposal account		
	Dr Accumulated depreciation with depreciation to date	1,000	
	Cr Disposals with depreciation to date		1,000
3	Account for disposal proceeds of old van/Purchase of new van		
	Dr Van account with total value ($2,200 cash + $1,000 p/e)	3,200	
	Cr Cash with cash paid (account not shown)		2,200
	Cr Disposals with part exchange amount		1,000
4	Calculate profit/loss on sale		
	Dr Statement of profit or loss with loss	100	
	Cr Disposals with loss (balancing figure on account)		100

3 Allowance for receivables

An allowance for receivables of $538 is required at the end of the year.
Total receivables = $10,760. Opening allowances $437.

Allowance for receivables

1 Bal c/f	538	Per TB	437
		Irrecoverable debts	101
	538		**538**
		Balance b/f	538

Irrecoverable debts expense

Per TB	1,791	Profit or loss	1,892
Allow for receivables	101		
	1,892		**1,892**

Sole trader accounts

		Dr	Cr
1	**Account for increase in allowance**		
	Dr Irrecoverable debts expense	101	
	Cr Allowance for receivables with balancing figure on this a/c		101
2	**Close irrecoverable debts expense to statement of profit or loss**		
	Dr Statement of profit or loss	1,892	
	Cr Irrecoverable debts expense with total charge for year		1,892

3 Other adjustments

Irrecoverable debts

Dr Irrecoverable debts expense	X
Cr RLCA	X

Depreciation expense

Dr Depreciation expense	X
Cr Accumulated depreciation	X

Accruals

Dr Expense account	X
Cr Accruals (SFP)	X

Prepayments

Dr Prepayments (SFP)	X
Cr Expense account	X

Sole trader accounts

Closing the books

After the final accounts have been prepared, the books are closed:

1. Transfer the balances on all statement of profit or loss accounts to the statement of profit or loss ledger.
2. Transfer the final balance on the statement of profit or loss account (the profit or loss) to the capital account.
3. Transfer the balance on the drawings account to the capital account.

Capital account

		B/f	8,000
3 Drawings	3,750	2 Profit	2,000
C/f	6,250		
	10,000		10,000
		B/f	6,250

This process ensures that income and expense accounts and the drawings account are 'cleared out' and start from a nil position in the new accounting period.

chapter 11

Partnership accounts

In this chapter

- Partnership agreements.
- Advantages and disadvantages of partnerships.
- Partnership accounts – overview.
- Partnership accounts.
- Profit appropriation.
- Other key points.
- Guaranteed minimum profit shares.
- Partnership financial statements.

Partnership agreements

Definition

A partnership is two or more individuals working together, normally with some agreement drawn up between them.

Partnership Agreement

= agreement, not necessarily written, which governs relationships between partners.

Matters normally included:

- Name of firm, type of business, duration
- Amounts of capital introduced
- Distribution of profits
- Drawings allowed
- Arrangements for dissolution
- Setting of disputes
- Preparation and audit of accounts.

Advantages and disadvantages of partnerships

Advantages of partnership	Disadvantages of partnership
- Business risk spread between partners. - Individual partners develop specific skills for partnership – not 'jack of all trades'. - Provides more capital for business. - Continuation of the business if one partner dies or retires.	- Disputes between partners e.g. on direction of business. - Joint and several liability – all partners liable for business debts, no matter which partner incurred them. - Discussion amongst partners may mean it takes longer to make business decisions.

Partnership accounts

Partnership accounts – overview

Statement of profit or loss – as for sole trader

↓

Profit divided between the partners in **appropriation account / statement of appropriation of profit**

↓

Share of profit credited to partners' **current accounts**

Long-term capital transactions shown in partner's **capital accounts**

Statement of financial position
- Assets and liabilities as for a sole trader
- Capital section includes partners' current and capital accounts

Partnership accounts

Capital accounts

- Show capital introduced into partnership.
- Only change when capital is amended (introduced or withdrawn, normally on change in partnership).
- Partners may receive notional interest on amount of capital invested in partnership.

Partners' Capital accounts

	Ant	Bee		Ant	Bee
			Balance b/f	5,000	10,000
Balance c/f	5,000	10,000			
	5,000	10,000		5,000	10,000

Current accounts

- Show current amount owing/owed between partnership and each partner.
- Receive profit share for year and show drawings made by each partner.

Partners' current accounts

	Ant	Bee		Ant	Bee
Drawings	2,500	11,000	Balance b/f	3,750	8,000
Balance c/f	6,250	2,000	Profit	5,000	5,000
	8,750	13,000		8,750	13,000

Partnership accounts

Profit appropriation account

- Shows split of profit for year between partners.
- Profit split depends on partnership agreement.

Appropriation account			
Share of profit		Net Profit	
Ant	5,000		
Bee	5,000		
	10,000		10,000

Statement of financial position presentation

- Partners' accounts shown separately on statement of financial position.

Partners' accounts	Capital	Current	Total
Ant	5,000	6,250	11,250
Bee	10,000	2,000	12,000
	15,000	**8,250**	**23,250**

Profit appropriation

May be up to four elements:
1 Interest on capital
2 Salaries
3 Interest on drawings
4 Profit share

Always calculate the profit share last.

Partners' accounts	Ant	Bee	Total
Interest on capital @ 8%	400	800	1,200
Salaries (assumed)	2,000	3,000	5,000
Interest on drawings @ 2%	(50)	(220)	(270)
Profit share 2:3	1,628	2,442	4,070
	3,978	6,022	10,000

Note: this example assumes drawings were made at the start of the year and so a full year's interest is charged.

Double entry:

Appropriation of profit: Ant and Bee partnership	Dr	Cr
1 Dr Statement of profit or loss	10,000	
Cr Appropriation account		10,000
2 Dr Appropriation account	10,000	
Cr Ant current account		3,978
Cr Bee current account		6,022

Other key points

Drawings	Partner makes loan to partnership	Partners' salaries
- May attract interest during the year. - Effectively means increase in profits for appropriation. - Interest is calculated from the date of withdrawal.	- Amount over and above capital. - Normally temporary. - Treat as if loan made by third party. - Interest therefore charged to statement of profit or loss.	- Are appropriation of profit (not an expense like employees' salaries). - Salaries are not necessarily withdrawn by partners.

Guaranteed minimum profit shares

- Some partnerships guarantee minimum profit share to some partners.
- Where profit insufficient to pay this, other partners make good in proportion to their profit-sharing ratio.

Example

- A, B and C share profits 1:2:3
- A has a guaranteed profit of $5,000
- If A's profit is only $2,500, then B and C make up $2,500 in ratio 2:3
- B pays $1,000 and C pays $1,500

Partnership accounts

Partnership financial statements

Prepare as follows:

Statement of profit or loss	Statement of financial position
• Prepare as for sole trader to net profit.	• Prepare as for sole trader for assets and liabilities.
• Calculate split of net profit per appropriation rules.	• Capital account of sole trader replaced with balances on partners' capital and current accounts.
• Transfer profit shares to partners' current accounts.	
• Deduct drawings from current accounts.	

Exam focus

The most complicated section of partnerships is the appropriation of profit. Remember that interest on capital, partner's salaries, interest on drawings and finally the profit share all form part of this calculation.

An exam question will not ask for full partnership accounts, but is likely to require a working showing the division of profit and possibly capital and current accounts.

chapter

12

Incomplete records

In this chapter
- Net asset approach.
- Using cost structures to find missing figures.
- Using ledger accounts to find missing figures.
- Incomplete records – question approach.

Incomplete records

Net asset approach

Find profit based on change in net assets over the year.

1. Prepare assets and liabilities of statement of financial position at the end of the year – that is to find net assets.
2. Prepare similar statement of financial position at the end of last year (normally given in the question).
3. Calculate difference between the two net assets figures.
4. Deduct capital introduced.
5. Add drawings.
6. This gives the profit for the year.

Statement of financial position	This year	Last year
Non-current assets	14,000	10,000
Receivables	12,100	6,000
Inventory	23,000	18,500
Cash and bank	15,000	14,500
Payables	(8,000)	(7,500)
Net assets	56,100	41,500
Increase in net assets		14,600
Less capital introduced in year		(5,000)
Add drawings for year		15,000
Profit for the year		24,600

You may be required to make adjustments to this year's statement of financial position figures:

Typical exam comment	Working
CA of non-current assets b/f was 15,000. New machine purchased for 6,000 and old machine with CV of 3,000 disposed of. Depreciation charge was 4,000.	**Non-current assets** CV b/f + Purchases in year − Disposals (at CV) − Depreciation for year = CV c/f 15,000 + 6,000 − 3,000 − 4,000 = 14,000
The balance on the receivables ledger control account (some questions state the list of unpaid invoices) was 12,300 which includes 200 of debts against which an allowance is required.	**Receivables** Amount per RLCA − Allowance for receivables = Net receivables on statement of financial position 12,300 − 200 = 12,100
The value of inventory from the year-end inventory count and valuation was 25,000 although a provision of 2,000 is required against some obsolete inventory.	**Inventory** Cost − Adjustment to NRV = Statement of financial position value 25,000 − 2,000 = 23,000

Incomplete records

Exam focus

Remember profit is being determined by finding the difference between two statement of financial position. The information provided may look complicated, but follow the procedure outlined above and you will be able to find the profit figure.

Using cost structures to find missing figures

Cost structures

Definition

Gross profit percentage

= profit made per $100 of sales expressed as a percentage

Mark up

= amount of profit added to cost to obtain the selling price. Often expressed as a percentage of cost

Examples

Jones applies a mark up of 40% to purchases. Sales for the year are $150,000. What is gross profit?

Exam focus

The examiner frequently comments that students confuse mark up and margin. You must be able to distinguish these terms.

	Gross profit percentage		Mark up	
Sales	10,000	100%	12,000	120%
Cost of sales	8,000	80%	10,000	100%
Gross profit	**2,000**	**20%**	**2,000**	**20%**

Gross profit percentage	Gross profit

Incomplete records

Sales	10,000	100%	
Cost of sales	8,000	80%	$150,000 \times \frac{40\%}{140\%} = 42,857$
Gross profit	2,000	20%	

Filbert achieves a 25% gross margin. What level of sales is needed to obtain $50,000 profit?

Gross profit

Sales	?	100%
Cost of sales	?	75%
Gross profit	50,000	25%

Sales

$50,000 \times \dfrac{100\%}{25\%} = 200,000$

Using ledger accounts to find missing figures

Cash and bank accounts

Need to complete both accounts to determine missing items e.g. amount of drawings.

Complete cash account first.

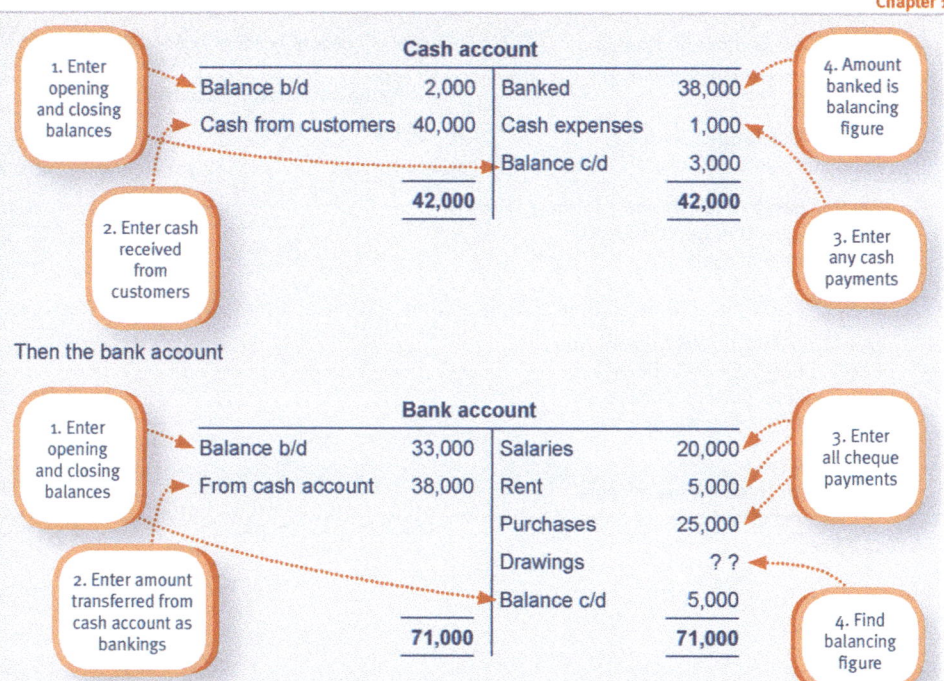

Incomplete records

In this case the missing figure of drawings can be determined as $16,000.

Receivables ledger control account

Can be used to find any one missing figure that would normally appear in the account.

Example

Balance b/d on control account was $12,000 and c/d = $16,000. Cash received from customers per bank was $40,000. What was the sales figure?

1. Construct the control account and insert the balances as given.

2. The balancing figure is sales at $44,000.

Receivables ledger control account

Balance b/d	12,000		
Sales	? ?	Cash received	40,000
		Balance c/d	16,000
	56,000		56,000

Payables ledger control account

Example

Balance b/d on control account was $7,000 and c/d = $5,000. Cash payments to suppliers per bank was $25,000. What was the purchases figure?

1. Construct the control account and insert the balances as given.

2. The balancing figure is purchases at $23,000.

Payables ledger control account

Payments to suppliers	25,000	Balance b/d	7,000
Balance c/d	5,000	Purchases	? ?
	30,000		30,000

Trading account and cost structures

Knowledge of the format of the trading account and the cost structure means we can find missing figures in this account.

Incomplete records

Procedure outlined below:

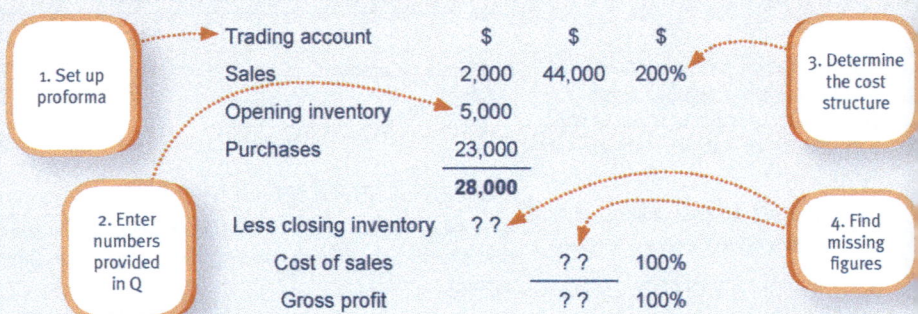

	$	$	$
Trading account			
Sales	2,000	44,000	200%
Opening inventory	5,000		
Purchases	23,000		
	28,000		
Less closing inventory	??		
Cost of sales		??	100%
Gross profit		??	100%

1. Set up proforma
2. Enter numbers provided in Q
3. Determine the cost structure
4. Find missing figures

Cost structure = 100% mark up on goods purchased.

Missing figures

Cost of sales = 50% of sales value (100% mark up) = 22,000

Gross profit = Sales less cost of sales = 22,000

Closing inventory = Cost of sales − Opening inventory − Purchases

= 22,000 − 5,000 − 23,000

= 6,000

Incomplete records – question approach

Summary of question approach below.

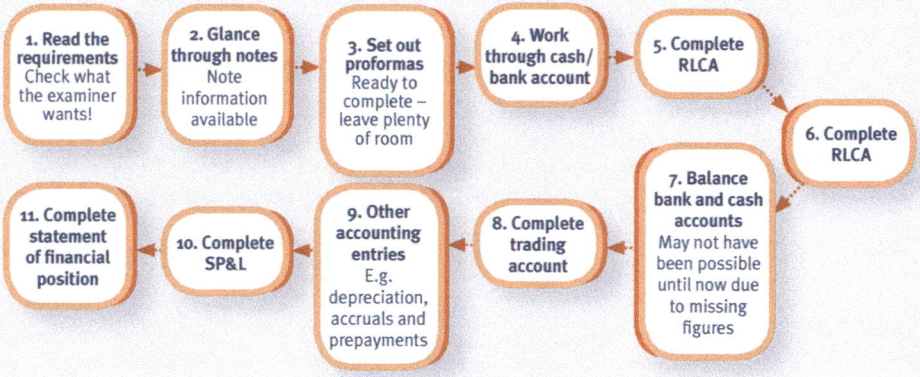

Incomplete records

Exam focus

Incomplete records questions appear to contain lots of data. The key to getting good marks is to work through this data methodically following the procedure above. If the statement of financial position doesn't balance then have a quick look at your workings for errors – but if none are obvious then move on. You may lose a mark but this is better than having too little time to complete the other questions in the examination.

Index

Index

A
Accounting 2
Accounting equation 2
Accruals 35, 70, 103
Allowance for receivables 74, 101
Appropriation account 110
Assets 2, 5
AVCO 82

B
Bank reconciliation 62
Books of original (or prime) entry 11
Break up basis 35
Business entity 35
Business entity concept 2

C
Capital 2, 5, 40
Cash payments cycle 14
Cash receipts cycle 16
Comparable 36
Conceptual Framework 37
Consistency 35
Continuous AVCO 82, 84
Control accounts 54
Credit purchase 7
Credit sale 7
Credit transactions 7
Current assets 41

D
Deferred income 72
Depreciation 43, 103
Depreciation expense 103
Discounts 12
Dishonoured cheques 63
Disposals of non-current assets 48
Double entry rules 6
Drawings 5, 112

Index

E
Errors 24, 26
Expenses 4
Extended trial balance 91

F
FIFO 82
Final accounts 96

G
General ledger 6, 11
Going concern 35
Gross margin 120

H
Historic cost 35

I
IAS 1 36
IAS 2 80
IAS 16 39
IAS 37 86
Imprest system 67
Income received in arrears 73
Incomplete records 115, 125
Inventory 80, 97
Irrecoverable debts 74, 75

J
Journal 18

L
Ledgers 11
Liabilities 2, 5
Liabilities and provisions 86

M
Mark up 119
Materiality 35

Index

N
Net asset approach 116
Net realisable value 80
Non-current asset disposals 99
Non-current assets 41

P
Part exchange 49
Partnership accounts 105, 108
Partnership agreements 106
Payables ledger 54
Payables ledger control account 54
Periodic AVCO 82, 84
Personal ledgers 11
Petty cash 66
Prepayments 71
Profit 4
Profit appropriation 111
Prudence 35
Purchases and sales tax 8

Purchases cycle 13

R
Receivables ledger 54
Receivables ledger control account 54
Reconciliation 56
Reducing balance 43
Relevant 36
Reliable 36
Residual value 43
Revenue 4
Revenue expenditure 40

S
Sales and sales tax 9
Sales cycle 15
Sales tax 7
Settlement discounts 12
Sole trader accounts 95
Statement of financial position 5

Statement of profit or loss 4
Straight line 43
Suppliers' statements 59
Suspense account 27

T
Trade discounts 12
Trading account 123
Trial balance 22

U
Understandable 36
Useful life 43
Users 34

Index